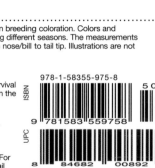

1. Barr Lake State Park
2. Rocky Mountain Arsenal National Wildlife Refuge
3. Wheat Ridge Greenbelt
4. City Park
5. Red Rocks Park
6. South Platte River Greenway
7. Cherry Creek State Park
8. Audubon Center & Chatfield State Park
9. Waterton Canyon
10. Roxborough State Park
11. Bear Creek Lake Park
12. Castlewood Canyon State Park
13. Genesee Mountain
14. Meyer Ranch

Denver Audubon inspires actions that protect birds, other wildlife, and their habitats through education, conservation, and research. We offer a variety of programs and field trips for schools, families, and adults at the Audubon Center at Chatfield and throughout the Denver region. For more information about all we offer, visit our website at **www.denveraudubon.org**.

For more information contact:

DENVER AUDUBON

Denver Audubon
9308 S. Wadsworth Blvd.
Littleton, CO 80128
303-973-9530
www.denveraudubon.org

Most illustrations show the adult male in breeding coloration. Colors and markings may be duller or absent during different seasons. The measurements denote the length of most animals from nose/bill to tail tip. Illustrations are not to scale.

Waterford Press publishes reference guides that introduce readers to nature observation, outdoor recreation and survival skills. Product information is featured on the website: **www.waterfordpress.com**.

Text & illustrations © 2014, 2022 Waterford Press Inc. All rights reserved. Cover image by Bob Stocker. To order or for information on custom published products please call 800-434-2555 or email orderdesk@waterfordpress.com. For permissions or to share comments email editor@waterfordpress.com.

ISBN 978-1-58355-975-8 $7.95 U.S.

Made in the USA

9 781583 559758   50795

8 84682 00892 5

10 9 8 7 6 5 4 3 2 1   2206101

A POCKET NATURALIST® GUIDE

DENVER BIRDS

A Folding Pocket Guide to Familiar Species

DENVER AUDUBON

(spine) DENVER BIRDS – A Folding Pocket Guide to Familiar Species

---

Pied-billed Grebe
Podilymbus podiceps
To 15 in. (38 cm)
White bill is banded in summer.

Western Grebe
Aechmophorus occidentalis
To 30 in. (75 cm)

Cackling Goose
Branta hutchinsii
To 34 in. (85 cm)
Distinguished from the Canada goose by its small size and shorter neck. Present all winter.

Canada Goose
Branta canadensis
To 45 in. (1.1 m)

Wood Duck
Aix sponsa To 20 in. (50 cm)

Blue-winged Teal
Spatula discors To 16 in. (40 cm)
Male has a white facial crescent.

Cinnamon Teal
Spatula cyanoptera To 17 in. (43 cm)

Mallard
Anas platyrhynchos To 28 in. (70 cm)

Green-winged Teal
Anas crecca To 16 in. (40 cm)

American Wigeon
Mareca americana To 23 in. (58 cm)

Northern Shoveler
Spatula clypeata To 20 in. (50 cm)
Note large spatulate bill.

Northern Pintail
Anas acuta To 30 in. (75 cm)

Gadwall
Mareca strepera To 21 in. (53 cm)

Redhead
Aythya americana To 22 in. (55 cm)

Bufflehead
Bucephala albeola To 15 in. (38 cm)

Ruddy Duck
Oxyura jamaicensis To 16 in. (40 cm)

Lesser Scaup
Aythya affinis To 18 in. (45 cm)

Common Goldeneye
Bucephala clangula To 20 in. (50 cm)

Ring-necked Duck
Aythya collaris To 18 in. (45 cm)
Bill has a white ring.

Common Merganser
Mergus merganser
To 27 in. (68 cm)

Double-crested Cormorant
Phalacrocorax auritus
To 3 ft. (90 cm)

American Coot
Fulica americana
To 16 in. (40 cm)

American White Pelican
Pelecanus erythrorhynchos
To 6 ft. (1.8 m)

White-faced Ibis
Plegadis chihi
To 25 in. (63 cm)

Great Blue Heron
Ardea herodias
To 4.5 ft. (1.4 m)

Snowy Egret
Egretta thula
To 26 in. (65 cm)
Note black bill and yellow feet.

Black-crowned Night-Heron
Nycticorax nycticorax
To 28 in. (70 cm)

American Avocet
Recurvirostra americana
To 20 in. (50 cm)

Spotted Sandpiper
Actitis macularius
To 8 in. (20 cm)

Wilson's Snipe
Gallinago delicata
To 12 in. (30 cm)

Long-billed Dowitcher
Limnodromus scolopaceus
To 12 in. (30 cm)

Lesser Yellowlegs
Tringa flavipes
To 10 in. (25 cm)
Call is a 1-3 note whistle.

Killdeer
Charadrius vociferus
To 12 in. (30 cm)
Note black breast bands.

Ring-billed Gull
Larus delawarensis
To 20 in. (50 cm)
Bill has a dark ring.

Franklin's Gull
Leucophaeus pipixcan
To 14 in. (35 cm)

California Gull
Larus californicus
To 23 in. (58 cm)
Has a black and red spot on its bill.

Long-eared Owl
Asio otus
To 16 in. (40 cm)
Ears are more closely set than those of the great horned owl.

Great Horned Owl
Bubo virginianus
To 25 in. (63 cm)
Call is a resonant – hoo-HOO-hoooo.

Barn Owl
Tyto alba
To 18 in. (45 cm)
Face is heart-shaped.

Eastern Screech-Owl
Megascops asio
To 9 in. (23 cm)
Call is a series of whistles.

Burrowing Owl
Athene cunicularia
To 9 in. (23 cm)

Downy Woodpecker
Dryobates pubescens
To 6 in. (15 cm)

Hairy Woodpecker
Dryobates villosus
To 10 in. (25 cm)
The similar downy woodpecker is smaller and has a shorter bill.

Northern Flicker
Colaptes auratus
To 13 in. (33 cm)
Wing and tail linings are yellow or red.

Mourning Dove
Zenaida macroura
To 13 in. (33 cm)

Rock Pigeon
Columba livia
To 13 in. (33 cm)
The common urban pigeon.

Eurasian Collared-Dove
Streptopelia decaocto
To 11 in. (28 cm)
Note dark band on nape.

Common Poorwill
Phalaenoptilus nuttallii
To 8 in. (20 cm)
Rhythmic call – poorwill, poorwill – is heard in the evening.

Common Nighthawk
Chordeiles minor
To 10 in. (25 cm)
Often seen for insects around street lights.

Black-chinned Hummingbird
Archilochus alexandri
To 3.5 in. (9 cm)
An increasing breeder.

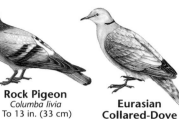

Broad-tailed Hummingbird
Selasphorus platycercus
To 4 in. (10 cm)

Rufous Hummingbird
Selasphorus rufus
To 4 in. (10 cm)

Belted Kingfisher
Megaceryle alcyon
To 14 in. (35 cm)

Chimney Swift
Chaetura pelagica
To 6 in. (15 cm)
Appears to beat wings alternately in flight.

White-throated Swift
Aeronautes saxatalis
To 7 in. (18 cm)
Note thin, pointed wings and white throat.

Red-tailed Hawk
Buteo jamaicensis
To 25 in. (63 cm)

Sharp-shinned Hawk
Accipiter striatus
To 14 in. (35 cm)
Note long, square-edged tail and striped breast.

Cooper's Hawk
Accipiter cooperii
To 20 in. (50 cm)
Crow-sized hawk has a long, rounded tail.

Light Morph

Ferruginous Hawk
Buteo regalis
To 25 in. (63 cm)
Key field mark is white unbanded tail.

Golden Eagle
Aquila chrysaetos
To 40 in. (1 m)

Bald Eagle
Haliaeetus leucocephalus
To 43 in. (1.1 m)

Light Morph

Swainson's Hawk
Buteo swainsoni
To 22 in. (55 cm)

Prairie Falcon
Falco mexicanus
To 20 in. (50 cm)
Note dark 'armpits.'

American Kestrel
Falco sparverius
To 12 in. (30 cm)
Note small size and blue wings.

Light Morph

Rough-legged Hawk
Buteo lagopus
To 24 in. (60 cm)
Note dark banded white tail and dark 'wrists'.

Peregrine Falcon
Falco peregrinus
To 21 in. (53 cm)

Turkey Vulture
Cathartes aura
To 32 in. (80 cm)
Note red head. Trailing half of wings are silvery.

Osprey
Pandion haliaetus
To 25 in. (63 cm)

Northern Harrier
Circus hudsonius
To 2 ft. (60 cm)
Hunts in marshes.

Say's Phoebe
Sayornis saya
To 8 in. (20 cm)
Bobs tail when perching.

Western Kingbird
Tyrannus verticalis
To 9 in. (23 cm)
Note yellowish belly and square-tipped tail.

Western Wood-Pewee
Contopus sordidulus
To 7 in. (18 cm)

Eastern Kingbird
Tyrannus tyrannus
To 8 in. (20 cm)

Ruby-crowned Kinglet
Regulus calendula
To 4 in. (10 cm)

Horned Lark
Eremophila alpestris
To 8 in. (20 cm)

Northern Shrike
Lanius borealis
To 11 in. (28 cm)
Note hooked bill and a black mask.

House Wren
Troglodytes aedon
To 5 in. (13 cm)

Canyon Wren
Catherpes mexicanus
To 6 in. (15 cm)

Tree Swallow
Tachycineta bicolor
To 6 in. (15 cm)

Cliff Swallow
Petrochelidon pyrrhonota
To 6 in. (15 cm)
Tail is square-edged.

Blue-gray Gnatcatcher
Polioptila caerulea
To 5 in. (13 cm)

Northern Rough-winged Swallow
Stelgidopteryx serripennis
To 6 in. (15 cm)
Note dusky throat.

Barn Swallow
Hirundo rustica
To 8 in. (20 cm)
Note deeply forked tail.

Violet-green Swallow
Tachycineta Thalassina
To 6 in. (15 cm)

White-breasted Nuthatch
Sitta carolinensis
To 6 in. (15 cm)

Pygmy Nuthatch
Sitta pygmaea
To 4 in. (10 cm)
Common in the foothills.

Red-breasted Nuthatch
Sitta canadensis
To 5 in. (13 cm)
Note two narrow, white wing bars.

Black-capped Chickadee
Poecile atricapillus
To 6 in. (15 cm)

Mountain Chickadee
Poecile gambeli
To 5 in. (13 cm)
Note white 'eyebrow'.

American Dipper
Cinclus mexicanus
To 9 in. (23 cm)

Bushtit
Psaltriparus minimus
To 4 in. (10 cm)
Small gray bird with brown ear patch.

Blue Jay
Cyanocitta cristata
To 12 in. (30 cm)

Woodhouse's Scrub-Jay
Aphelocoma woodhouseii
To 13 in. (33 cm)

Common Raven
Corvus corax
To 27 in. (68 cm)
Call is a hoarse croak.

American Crow
Corvus brachyrhynchos
To 22 in. (55 cm)
Call is a distinct *caw*.

Steller's Jay
Cyanocitta stelleri
To 14 in. (35 cm)

Common Grackle
Quiscalus quiscula
To 12 in. (30 cm)

Clark's Nutcracker
Nucifraga columbiana
To 13 in. (33 cm)

American Robin
Turdus migratorius
To 11 in. (28 cm)

Western Bluebird
Sialia mexicana
To 7 in. (18 cm)

Mountain Bluebird
Sialia currucoides
To 7 in. (18 cm)

Gray Catbird
Dumetella carolinensis
To 9 in. (23 cm)
Note black cap and reddish undertail feathers.

Townsend's Solitaire
Myadestes townsendi
To 9 in. (23 cm)
Gray bird has a white eye ring and buffy wing patches.

Cedar Waxwing
Bombycilla cedrorum
To 8 in. (20 cm)
Red wing marks look like waxy droplets.

Black-billed Magpie
Pica hudsonia
To 22 in. (55 cm)

Western Tanager
Piranga ludoviciana
To 7 in. (18 cm)

Red-winged Blackbird
Agelaius phoeniceus
To 10 in. (25 cm)

Brewer's Blackbird
Euphagus cyanocephalus
To 10 in. (25 cm)

European Starling
Sturnus vulgaris
To 8 in. (20 cm)

Brown-headed Cowbird
Molothrus ater
To 8 in. (20 cm)

Western Meadowlark
Sturnella neglecta
To 12 in. (30 cm)

Yellow-headed Blackbird
Xanthocephalus xanthocephalus
To 11 in. (28 cm)

Bullock's Oriole
Icterus bullockii
To 8 in. (20 cm)

Yellow-breasted Chat
Icteria virens
To 7 in. (18 cm)

Common Yellowthroat
Geothlypis trichas
To 6 in. (15 cm)

Yellow-rumped Warbler
Setophaga coronata
To 6 in. (15 cm)
Note yellow on rump and crown. Throat is yellow or white.

Orange-crowned Warbler
Leiothlypis celata
To 6 in. (15 cm)

Virginia's Warbler
Oreothlypis virginiae
To 4.5 in. (11 cm)
Note prominent white eye ring and yellow undertail.

MacGillivray's Warbler
Geothlypis tolmiei
To 5 in. (13 cm)
Note gray hood and broken eye ring.

Wilson's Warbler
Cardellina pusilla
To 5 in. (13 cm)
Note black crown.

Yellow Warbler
Setophaga petechia
To 5 in. (13 cm)

Lesser Goldfinch
Spinus psaltria
To 4.5 in. (11 cm)

American Goldfinch
Spinus tristis
To 5 in. (13 cm)

Pine Siskin
Spinus pinus
To 5 in. (13 cm)

Black-headed Grosbeak
Pheucticus melanocephalus
To 8 in. (20 cm)

Chipping Sparrow
Spizella passerina
To 8 in. (20 cm)
Note chestnut cap.

American Tree Sparrow
Spizelloides arborea
To 7 in. (18 cm)
Note chestnut cap and small breast spot.

White-crowned Sparrow
Zonotrichia leucophrys
To 7 in. (18 cm)
White crown is bordered by black stripes.

Song Sparrow
Melospiza melodia
To 7 in. (18 cm)
Note central breast spot.

Lazuli Bunting
Passerina amoena
To 6 in. (15 cm)

Lark Bunting
Calamospiza melanocorys
To 7 in. (18 cm)
Colorado's state bird.

Spotted Towhee
Pipilo maculatus
To 8 in. (20 cm)

Green-tailed Towhee
Pipilo chlorurus
To 7 in. (18 cm)

House Sparrow
Passer domesticus
To 6 in. (15 cm)

House Finch
Haemorhous mexicanus
To 6 in. (15 cm)

Slate-colored Race

Oregon Race

Pink-sided Race

Gray-headed Race

Dark-eyed Junco
Junco hyemalis To 7 in. (18 cm)
Four related 'races' all have a dark hood and light outer tail feathers.